ANAHEIM DUCKS

By K.C. Kelley

The Child's World

THE CHILD'S WORLD®
1980 Lookout Drive • Mankato, MN 56003-1705
800-599-READ • www.childsworld.com

ACKNOWLEDGMENTS
The Child's World®: Mary Berendes, Publishing Director
Shoreline Publishing Group, LLC: James Buckley, Jr.,
 Production Director
The Design Lab: Gregory Lindholm, Design and
 Page Production

PHOTOS
Cover: Getty Images
Interior: AP/Wide World: 5, 6, 10, 12, 16, 21, 22, 24 (3),
 26, 27; Getty: 9, 13, 18

**LIBRARY OF CONGRESS
CATALOGING-IN-PUBLICATION DATA**
Kelley, K. C.
 Anaheim Ducks / by K. C. Kelley.
  p. cm.
 Includes bibliographical references and index.
 ISBN 978-1-60253-437-7 (library bound : alk. paper)
 1. Anaheim Ducks (Hockey Team)—History—Juvenile
literature. 2. Hockey teams—California—Anaheim—History—
Juvenile literature. 3. Hockey—California—Anaheim—History—
Juvenile literature. I. Title.

 GV848.A53K45 2010
 796.962'640979496—dc22

 2010015292

Printed in the United States of America
Mankato, Minnesota
July 2010
F11538

TABLE OF CONTENTS

GO, DUCKS!

The Anaheim Ducks are the only sports team that started thanks to a movie. And like a good movie, the team has given its fans lots of thrills and chills over the years. The Ducks are one of the best young teams in the National Hockey League (NHL). Their fans are watching eagerly for them to fly to the top again! Let's meet the Ducks!

4

Ducks star Ryan Getzlaf celebrates another big goal!

Great save! Ducks goalie Jonas Hiller blocks this shot by Jeff Halpern of the Tampa Bay Lightning.

WHO ARE THE ANAHEIM DUCKS?

The Anaheim Ducks are one of 30 teams in the NHL. The NHL includes the Eastern Conference and Western Conference. The Ducks play in the Pacific Division of the Western Conference. The playoffs end with the winners of the Eastern and Western conferences facing off. The champion wins the **Stanley Cup**. The Ducks have won one Stanley Cup.

WHERE THEY CAME FROM

The Ducks began playing in 1993. They were first named the Anaheim Mighty Ducks. The name came from a movie about a young hockey team. Their mascot was a giant duck named Wild Wing! The players took a lot of kidding about the name, but they proved to be tougher than most ducks! In 2006, the team changed owners. The new owners dropped the "Mighty" part of the name. It must have worked. The team won the Stanley Cup in its first Mighty-less season!

Here's Wild Wing wearing the team's original Mighty Ducks uniform at a 1994 game.

9

Jonas Hiller of the Ducks keeps this rival Kings player from scoring.

WHO THEY PLAY

The Anaheim Ducks play 82 games each season. They play all the other teams in their division six times. The other Pacific Division teams are the Dallas Stars, the Los Angeles Kings, the Phoenix Coyotes, and the San Jose Sharks. The Ducks and the Kings are fierce **rivals**. The Ducks also play other teams in the Western and Eastern Conferences.

WHERE THEY PLAY

The Ducks play their home games in the Honda Center. The **arena** has been the team's only home. However, the arena has an unofficial name among fans. Where do ducks spend a lot of their time? Why, a pond of course! Many fans still fondly flock to the Pond to watch their Ducks.

It's not wet, but fans call the Honda Center by its nickname: The Pond.

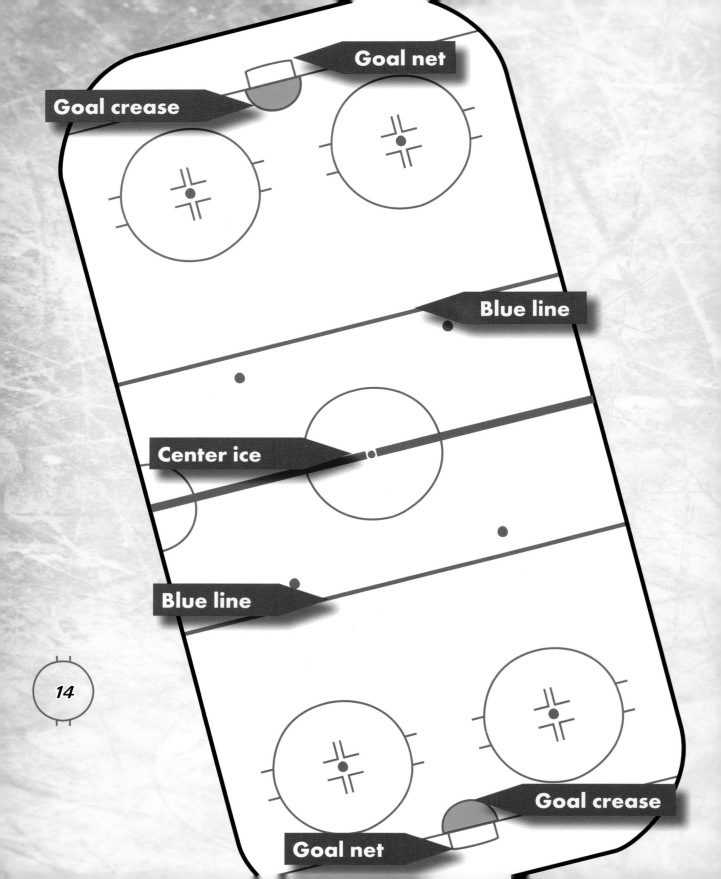

Goal net

Goal crease

Blue line

Center ice

Blue line

14

Goal crease

Goal net

THE HOCKEY RINK

Hockey games are played on a sheet of ice called a rink. It is a rounded rectangle. NHL rinks are 200 feet (61 m) long and 85 feet (26 m) wide. Wooden boards surround the entire rink. Clear plastic panels are on top of the boards so fans can see the action and be protected from flying **pucks**. Netting is hung above the seats at each end of the rink to catch any wild pucks. The goal nets are near each end of the rink. Each net is four feet (1.2 m) high and six feet (1.8 m) wide. A red line marks the center of the ice. Blue lines mark each team's defensive zone.

THE PUCK

An NHL puck is made of very hard rubber. The disk is three inches (76 mm) wide and 1 inch (25 mm) thick. It weighs about 6 ounces (170 g). It's black so it's easy to see on the ice. Many pucks are used during a game, because some fly into the stands.

15

BIG DAYS!

The Ducks have had many great seasons in their long history. Here are two of the greatest:

1997: The Ducks made the playoffs for the first time. In Game 4, Paul Kariya (kuh-REE-yuh) scored on a long goal to beat the Phoenix Coyotes in overtime.

2003: The Mighty Ducks were a surpise Western Conference champion. They made the Stanley Cup Finals, but lost to the New Jersey Devils.

2007: The Ducks won it all! Anaheim beat the Ottawa Senators to earn their first Stanley Cup trophy!

17

Hockey players never touch the Stanley Cup until they have actually won it. Here's Teemu Selanne with the trophy in 2007.

Ouch! Jamie Pushor of the Ducks gets checked by Dallas Drake of the Phoenix Coyotes in this 1998 game.

TOUGH DAYS!

Not every season can end with a Stanley Cup championship. Here are some of the toughest seasons in the Ducks' history.

1997: After coach Ron Wilson led the team to the playoffs for the first time, he was fired. Fans were shocked and players were surprised. Wilson had been very popular . . . except with team owners.

1997–98: The Ducks won only 26 games—the second-worst season in team history.

2003: Paul Kariya was a popular and successful star for the Ducks. However, he shocked his fans by leaving the team to sign with the Colorado Avalanche. It was a sad day for Anaheim.

19

MEET THE FANS

When your team is called the Ducks, you get to have a little fun. Fans at Ducks games wear hats with duck bills. They wear the team's snarling duck logo on their shirts. In the team's early days, fans even blew on duck calls during games. The Ducks are the only pro team in Orange County, a large area south of Los Angeles, California. Fans from all over the county flock to see their local heroes.

Ducks star Teemu Selanne greeted happy fans celebrating the team's 2007 Stanley Cup championship.

High-scoring forward: Teemu Selanne
is one of the most beloved Ducks.

HEROES THEN...

Though they're a newer team, the Ducks still have had their share of star players. Perhaps the best player in their early seasons was left **wing** Paul Kariya. He scored many key goals for the team. In 1995, he was joined by high-scoring **center** Teemu Selanne from Finland. While in Anaheim, Selanne twice led the NHL in goals. **Defenseman** Scott Niedermayer wrapped up his great career by giving the Ducks **veteran** leadership through 2010. One of the team's most beloved players was goalie Guy Hebert (GEE eh-BEAR). He was the first player to be made a Mighty Duck. He "tended the nets" for eight seasons. Jean-Sebastian Giguere (zhih-GAYR) was the goalie during the team's Stanley Cup run.

HEROES NOW...

The Ducks' biggest superstar now is high-scoring center Ryan Getzlaf. He's only in his fifth NHL season and he'll be a star for years. Right wing Corey Perry makes a powerful scoring team with Getzlaf. Veteran center Saku Koivu from Finland joined the team in 2009. He was a star for many years with the Montreal Canadiens. The Ducks defense is led by Ryan Whitney and James Wisniewski. Anaheim also has a great goalie, young Swiss star Jonas Hiller.

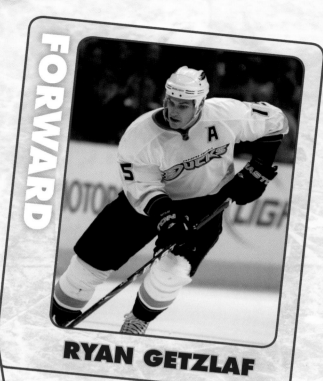

FORWARD

RYAN GETZLAF

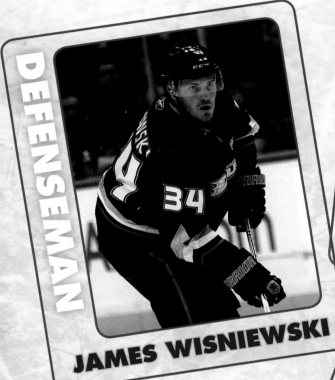

DEFENSEMAN

JAMES WISNIEWSKI

GOALIE

JONAS HILLER

25

GEARING UP

Hockey players wear short pants and a jersey called a "sweater." Underneath, they wear lots of pads to protect themselves. They also wear padded gloves and a hard plastic helmet. They wear special ice hockey skates with razor-sharp blades. They carry a stick to handle the puck.

Goalies wear special gloves to help them block and catch shots. They have extra padding on their legs, chest, and arms. They also wear special decorated helmets and use a larger stick.

26

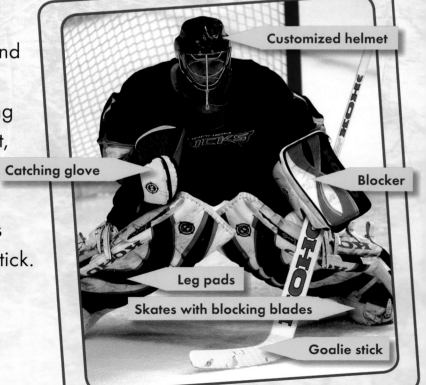

Customized helmet

Catching glove

Blocker

Leg pads

Skates with blocking blades

Goalie stick

Helmet

Face shield

Shoulder pads

Sweater

Gloves

Knee pads

Shin guards

Stick

Skates

27

SPORTS STATS

Here are some all-time
career records for the
Anaheim Ducks.
All the stats are through
the 2009–2010 season.

HOT SHOTS

GOALS

These players have scored the most
career goals for the Ducks.

PLAYER	GOALS
Teemu Selanne*	379
Paul Kariya	300

PERFECT PASSERS

ASSISTS

These players have the most career
assists on the team.

PLAYER	ASSISTS
Teemu Selanne *	412
Paul Kariya	369

BIG SCORES!

POINTS

These players have the most points,
a combination of goals and assists.

PLAYER	POINTS
Teemu Selanne*	791
Paul Kariya	669

28

GOALS AGAINST AVERAGE

SUPER SAVERS

These Anaheim goalies have allowed the fewest goals per game in their career.

PLAYER	GAA
Jean-Sebastian Giguere	2.47
Guy Hebert	2.75

CAREER PLUS-MINUS

PLAYER POSITIVE

These players have the best **plus-minus** in Ducks history.

PLAYER	PLUS-MINUS
Teemu Selanne *	+117
Ryan Getzlaf*	+64

COACHES

FROM THE BENCH

These coaches have the most wins in Ducks history.

COACH	WINS
Randy Carlyle*	219

29

* Active through 2009–2010

GLOSSARY

arena an indoor place for sports

center a hockey position at the middle of the forward, offensive line

defenseman a player who takes a position closest to his own goal, to keep the puck out

plus-minus a player gets a plus one for being on the ice when their team scores a goal, and a minus one when the other team scores a goal; the total of these pluses and minuses creates this stat. The better players always have high plus ratings

puck the hard, frozen rubber disk used when playing hockey

rivals teams that play each other often and with great intensity

Stanley Cup the trophy awarded each year to the winner of the National Hockey League championship

veteran an athlete who has been a pro for many years

wing a hockey position on the outside left or right of the forward line

FIND OUT MORE

BOOKS

Banks, Kerry. *Teemu Selanne*. Vancouver: Greystone Books, 2003.

Shea, Therese. *Hockey Stars*. Danbury, CT: Children's Press, 2007.

Thomas, Kelly, and John Kicksee. *Inside Hockey!: The Legends, Facts, and Feats that Made the Game*. Toronto: Maple Leaf Press, 2008.

WEB SITES

Visit our Web page for links about the Anaheim Ducks and other pro hockey teams.

childsworld.com/links

Note to Parents, Teachers, and Librarians: We routinely verify our Web links to make sure they are safe, active sites—so encourage your readers to check them out!

31

INDEX

ABOUT THE AUTHOR

K.C. Kelley has written dozens of books on sports for young readers. He has also been a youth baseball and soccer coach. When he was a kid, he spent a lot of time rooting for the Los Angeles Kings and playing street hockey.